MUSIC NUMBERS

A Novel Approach to the Note Relationships
of
Scales and Chords
for
Guitar and Keyboard

Shanny
Nadudvary

I.S.B.N.

978-0-9736193-8-6

Copyright S. Nadudvary 2012.

To Mom, for all of her help.

CONTENTS

<< PREFACE >>... 7
<< WHAT ARE MUSIC NUMBERS? >>................... 8
<< THE MUSIC ALPHABET >>........................... 9
<< MUSIC NUMBERS >>................................. 10
<< HYMN EXAMPLE >>................................. 11
<< GENERAL CHORD CODES >>....................... 13
<< INTRODUCTION >>.................................. 15
<< THE MUSIC NUMBER SYSTEM >>................. 16
<< WHAT ARE MODES? AND WHY? >>................ 18
<< ABOUT THE DIAGRAMS >>......................... 19
<< BOOGIE WOOGIE >>................................ 24
<< PENTATONIC SCALE >>............................. 25
<< GUITAR/KEYBOARD CORRELATION >>............ 27
<< LIST of SCALE CODES >>.......................... 28

MUSIC NUMBERS CHORDS for the --KEYBOARD--

<< PREFACE >>

As far back as 1584, Chu Tsai-yu, who was a prince of the Ming Dynasty in China, published the set of twelve named notes we use today. In this book, we number the notes from 0 through 11.

Traditionally, music has been defined by the Music Alphabet. Music *Numbers* are designed to enhance traditional teaching methods but may be used independently as well.

Although scales and chord structures commonly overwhelm and confuse a beginner, Music Numbers are a way of unraveling them. Music Numbers, or MNs, were created by the author merging a fundamental of physics with a desire to understand music.

<< WHAT ARE MUSIC NUMBERS? >>

Music Numbers are a tool of empowerment for analyzing and applying musical notes.

A keyboard, such as a piano or organ, can be thought of as a single line of notes represented by black keys and white keys. The white keys are laid out beside one another; the black keys are laid inside of the white keys. When sounding both the black and white keys in a linear sequence there are twelve different distinct notes before they are repeated on another register. Music Numbers are designed to help you find the harmonic sequences within. The notes in one set are the same for all the other sets.

A chord is a combination of notes played simultaneously. If the notes of a chord are played individually, and in sequence, they are called an arpeggio (ahr-pej-ee-oh). This section simplifies the chords so they may reasonably be applied to keyboards.

<< THE MUSIC ALPHABET >>

Guitar chords are complex creatures on the guitar. To apply a MN chord code to any key on the keyboard, start from a desired key and plug in the appropriate chord code. That's basically it, in a nutshell.

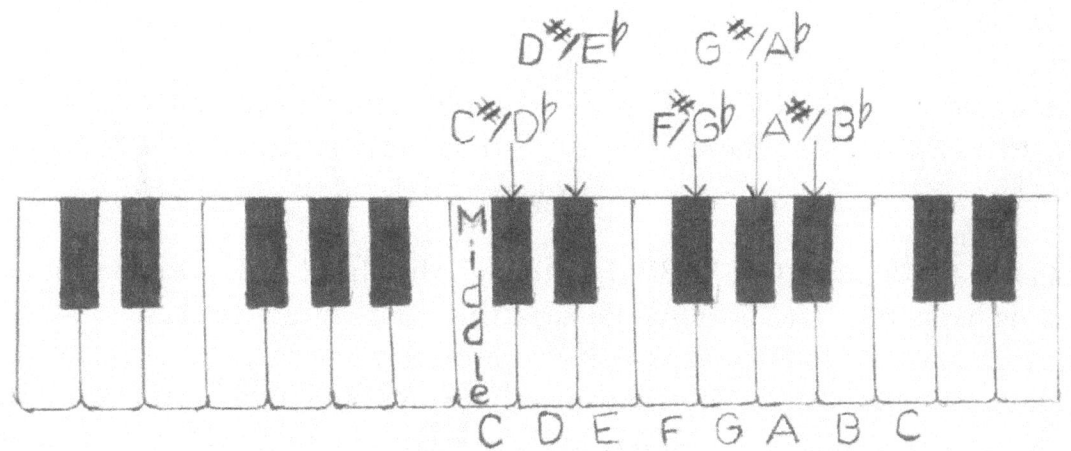

Note Key Music Alphabet

Note: <u>white</u> keys bear <u>fixed</u> letter names of the alphabet, <u>A through G</u>. For example, from Middle C: C-D-E-F-G-A-B-C. In our illustration, the beginning note is C, and the ending note, a higher-pitched C.

<< MUSIC NUMBERS >>

GIVEN: *Before continuing it is recommended that the reader/ student can* **identify** *the different keys on the keyboard by their* **Music Alphabet** *names. The advantage of this will be the ability to read guitar chords from books for playing on a keyboard.*

Applying Music Numbers to chords is comparable to a game of "connecting the dots." The General Chord Codes at the end of this section shows how simple it really is. For example, to find the notes for a Major chord, look at the MN code listed for Major chords on the chart, namely: 0-4-7. Start on a note as ZERO, and play it, along with the 4th and the 7th numbered notes in the line.

For example, start with Middle C as ZERO and count up the keys, both black and white, to sound the MN chord code: 0-4-7-0 (C-E-G-C) Note the added ZERO. Using the F key as ZERO, play the same chord code: 0-4-7-0 (F-A-C-F).

Play G7: 0-4-7-**10**, with G as ZERO. Although the chord codes used in these three positions happen to land on all-white keys, this is not always the case. Some chord codes may have too many notes to play comfortably at once. Use discretion. Try sounding the chords' notes in various combinations, and individually too. Although outside the scope of this book, there are lessons on the INTERNET about creating effects with chords, playing with two hands, opening them up, etc.

Traditionally, chords are written for the guitar with a Music Alphabet named note followed by a signifier. A Music Alphabet named chord with no signifier is assumed to be a Major chord. At the end of this section is a chart listing the chords by their names, signifiers, and Music Numbers. Each chord code can be applied to any note. For example: With G_m, G is ZERO. The Minor signifier gives us the chord code from the chart, as: 0-3-7, to be the relative notes sounded. All chords can be found this way. The secret to Music Numbers is to count from ZERO, no matter where you start.

<< HYMN EXAMPLE >>

Swing Low Sweet Chariot
Chords illustrated

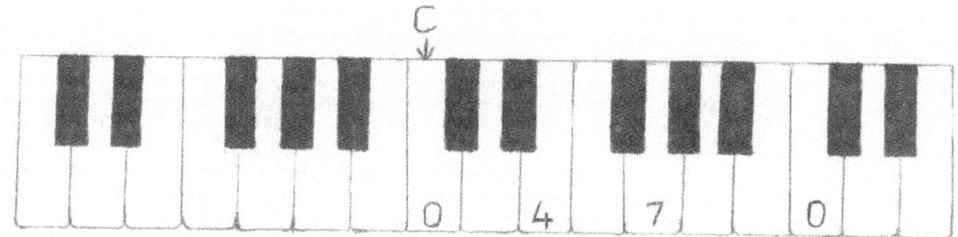

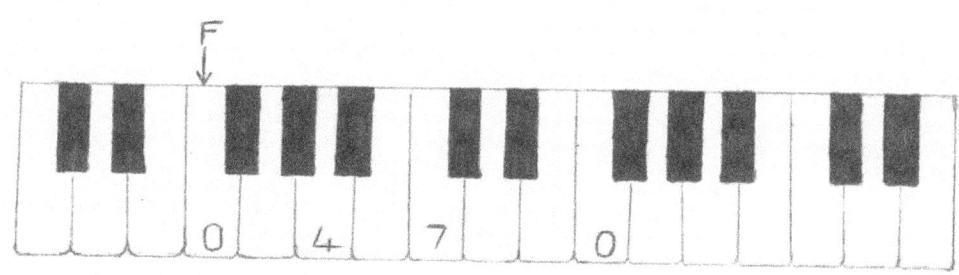

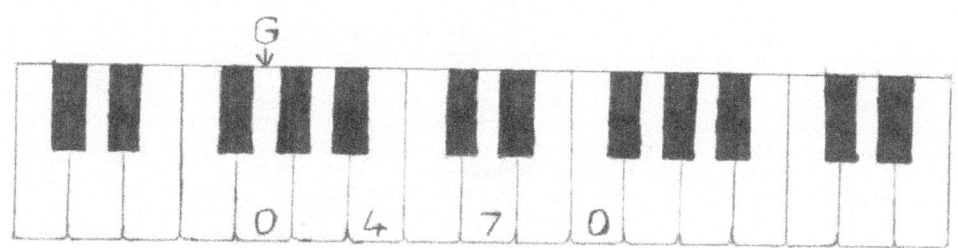

SWING LOW SWEET CHARIOT

```
        G           C         F       C
Ref:  SWING LOW SWEET CHARIOT
           C                      G
      COMING FOR TO CARRY ME HOME
             C          F
      SWING LOW SWEET CHARIOT
           C         G         C
      COMING FOR TO CARRY ME HOME

         C                         F          C
1)   LOOKED OVER JORDAN WHAT DID I SEE
                                G
     COMING FOR TO CARRY ME HOME
       C                 F              C
     A BAND OF ANGELS WAITING THERE FOR ME
              G         C
     COME FOR TO CARRY ME HOME (Chorus)


        C                       F        C
2) WHEN IT'S TIME TO LAY DOWN FOR REST
       C                  G
     COME FOR TO CARRY ME HOME
              C                   F         C
     MAY THE ANGELS WINGS PROTECT OUR NEST
              G         C
     COME FOR TO CARRY ME HOME (Chorus)
```

Guitar chords are written in many songbooks. Now it's simple to analyze them for playing on the keyboard.

<< GENERAL CHORD CODES >>

TYPE	SIGNIFIER	MUSIC NUMBERS
Major	M/none	0-4-7(-0)
Minor	m	0-3-7(-0)
Diminished	*7	0-3-6-9(-0)
Augmented	+5	0-4-8(-0)
Seventh	7	0-4-7-10(-0)
Minor Seventh	m7	0-3-7-10(-0)
Seventh Augmented Fifth	7+5	0-4-8-10(-0)
Seventh Flat Fifth	7-5	0-4-6-10(-0)
Major Seventh	M7	0-4-7-11(-0)
Major Seventh Flat Third	mM7	0-3-7-11(-0)
Minor Seventh Flat Fifth	m7-5	0-3-6-10(-0)
Seventh Suspended Fourth	sus7	0-5-7-10(-0)
Sixth	6	0-4-7-9(-0)
Minor Sixth	m6	0-3-7-9(-0)
Ninth	9	0-2-4-7-10(-0)
Minor Ninth	m9	0-2-3-7-10(-0)
Major Ninth	M9	0-2-4-7-11(-0)
Ninth Augmented Fifth	9+5	0-2-4-8-10(-0)
Ninth Flat Fifth	9-5	0-2-4-6-10(-0)
Seventh Flat Ninth	7-9	0-1-4-7-10(-0)
Augmented Ninth	+9	0-3-4-7-10(-0)
Sixth/Ninth	6/9	0-2-4-7-9(-0)
Eleventh	11	0-2-4-5-7-10(-0)
Augmented Eleventh	+11	0-2-4-6-7-10(-0)
Thirteenth	M13	0-2-4-7-9-10(-0)
Thirteenth Flat Ninth	13-9	0-1-4-7-9-10(-0)

MUSIC NUMBERS
SCALES
for
-- GUITAR --

<< INTRODUCTION >>

Guitar strings are spaced to conform to the human hand. After learning the Music Number technique, many musical possibilities may be had.

<< THE MUSIC NUMBER SYSTEM >>

Music Numbers name the notes ZERO through to eleven, starting to count from ZERO, *instead* of the traditional number ONE. The reasoning is, that if you start on the number ONE and count up five notes, you will be on a note numbered six, whereas, if you start on ZERO and count up five notes, the note will be numbered five.

Instead of counting beyond eleven, the set is repeated: **0**-1-2-3-4-5-6-7-8-9-10-11-**0**-1-2-3-4-5-6-7-8... To count downwards, count backwards. Scale sequences, and their relatives, are comprised of subsets within.

By placing ZERO at any selected position, Music Numbers can be used to designate the relevant notes to that position, with each MN equalling one fret space on the guitar.

Here's something to sleep on:
Imagine being without gravity on the landing of a staircase. There are eleven steps up, and eleven steps down to other landings. Eleven steps up, eleven steps down; then other landings with steps up and steps down. This go on and on into infinity.

The landings are ZEROs. They make a tonal sound: "Hmmmm... "As you go up the stairs, the tone gets higher. Descending, and the tone gets lower. When you arrive on another landing you find the same tone you started with at a higher or lower frequency, or pitch level. Go up and down the stairs having fun with the sounds, imaginary or not; take one or two steps at a time, jump around. Not only are you weightless, you are also as fast as thought.

Changing the steps into frets for the guitar, our landing becomes a fret on a string labelled Zero, to plot Mode One (coming up). The ZERO in Mode One is the root key. Note: the note spacing for all root keys is identical. Once a root key is defined so are all of that note's relatives. The fret spacing for Mode One is: 0-2-4-5-7-9-11-0, or, Zero- up 2 frets -up 2- up 1- up 2- up 2- up 2- up 1.
  0-2-4-5-7-9-11-0
  0-2-2-1-2-2- 2-1.

Remembering little number codes will help you identify note locations.

Scales represent notes that sound extremely well beside one another.

What a pleasant way to start learning music theory.

As time passes, thought is applied, and practise takes place; be amazed at the flower of understanding.

<< WHAT ARE MODES? AND WHY? >>

A sequence of notes known as a scale is used as the basis for a composition. Mode One (doe-ray-me-fa-so-la-tea-doe) starts on the first note of this sequence, Mode Two on the second note (ray-me-fa-so-la-tea-doe-ray), Mode Three on the third and so on, still using the same note sequence. Modes are like moods. Moods surround a person; modes surround a note. Thus, we need to choose a note to have as our center. This note is also called our root or key. Using MNs, we define this anchoring note as ZERO in Mode One. The other notes from Mode One provide ambience around it. By starting on different notes within Mode One, the other modes are defined. It is basically that simple.

<< ABOUT THE DIAGRAMS >>

Hint: The object here is to get an overview of the system. Music Numbers can be moved as a unit, whereas Music Alphabet names are fixed.

To illustrate: under Mode One on the following list and chart are its subsidiary modes with MNs for some example starting keys. Referring from the left, go across:

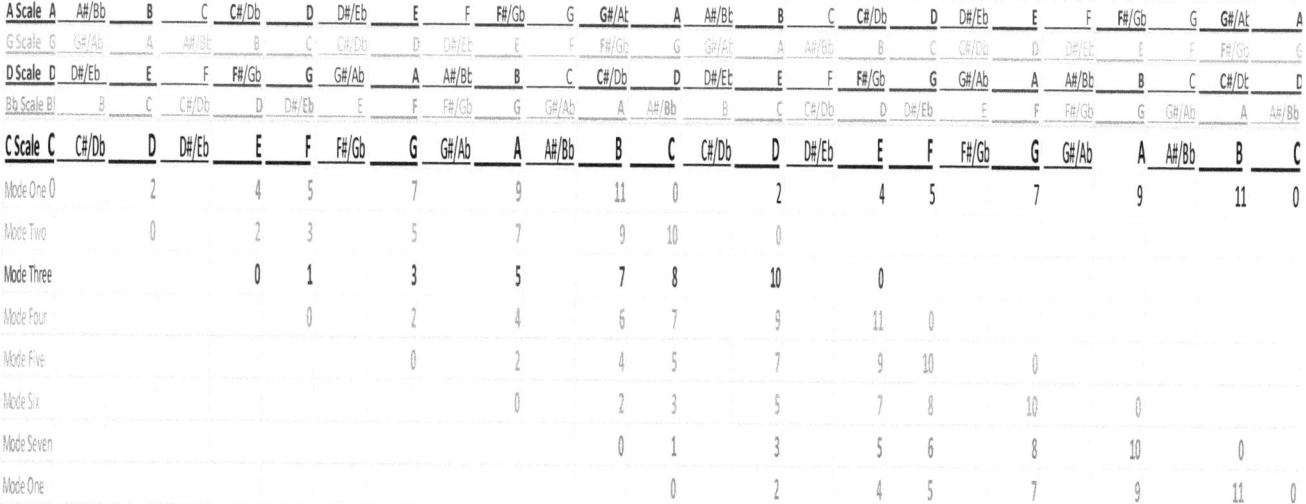

Examples: MNs with Music Alphabet

With seven different notes in Mode One, we can find the other modes, by numbering each note independently from Zero.

MNs across the six strings on any fret can be counted as: 0-5-10-3-7-0.

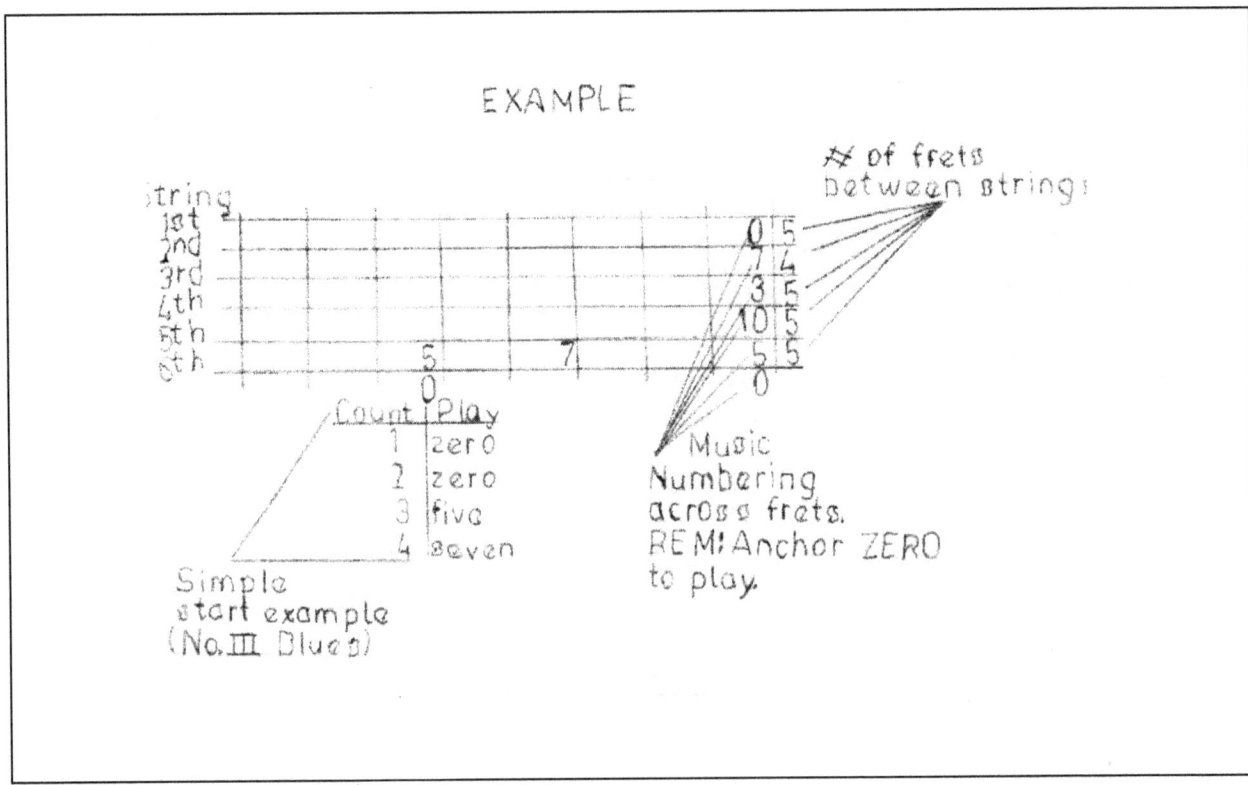

a) It makes sense to be able to start from alternative positions. By knowing how the strings are spaced, you can match Music Numbers to any fret position. Going up and down the fingerboard, MNs remain the same.

b) The following diagrams show an arbitrary portion of the fingerboard. Practice starting on different frets. Letters beside the MNs are for suggested fingering:

I -- Index
M -- Middle
R -- Ring
L -- Little

Note that Music Numbers on the top and bottom strings correspond.

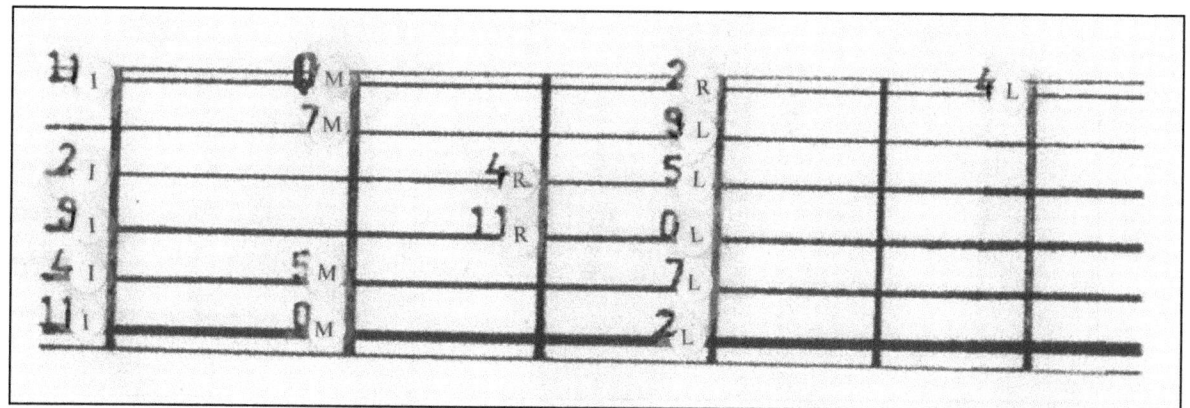

Mode One

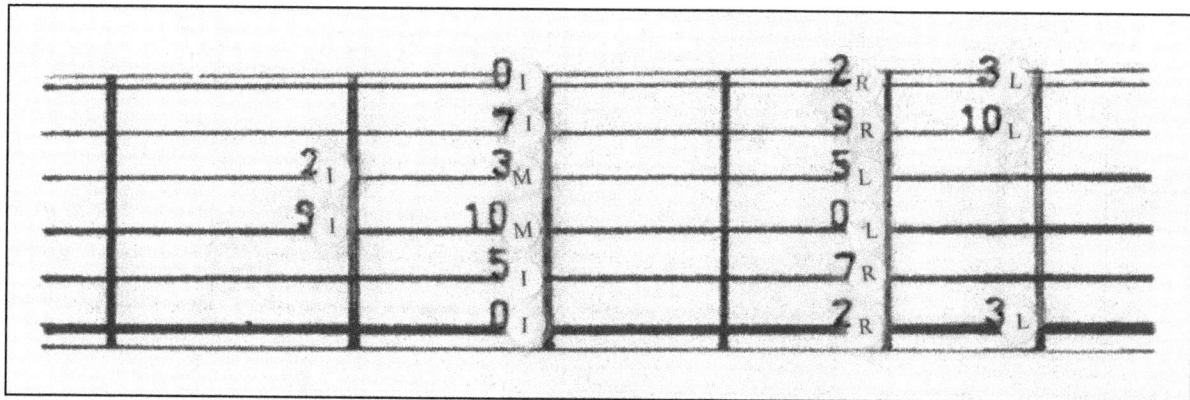

Mode Two

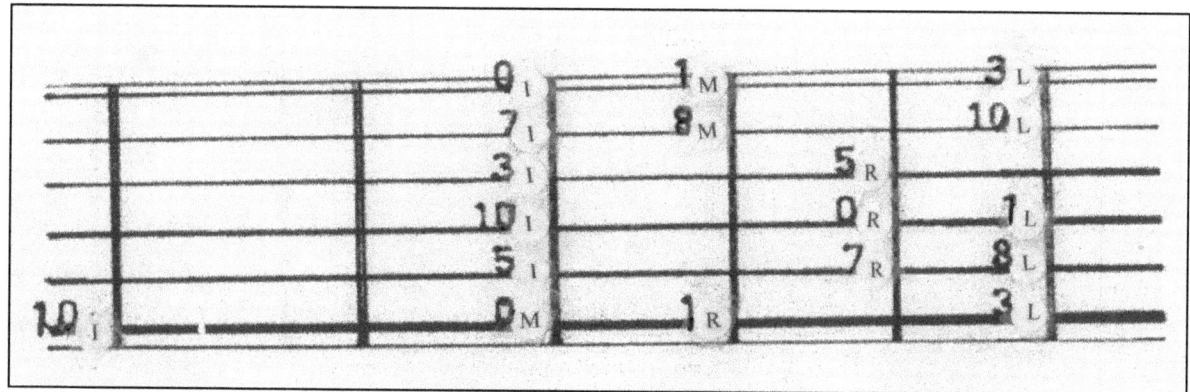

Mode Three

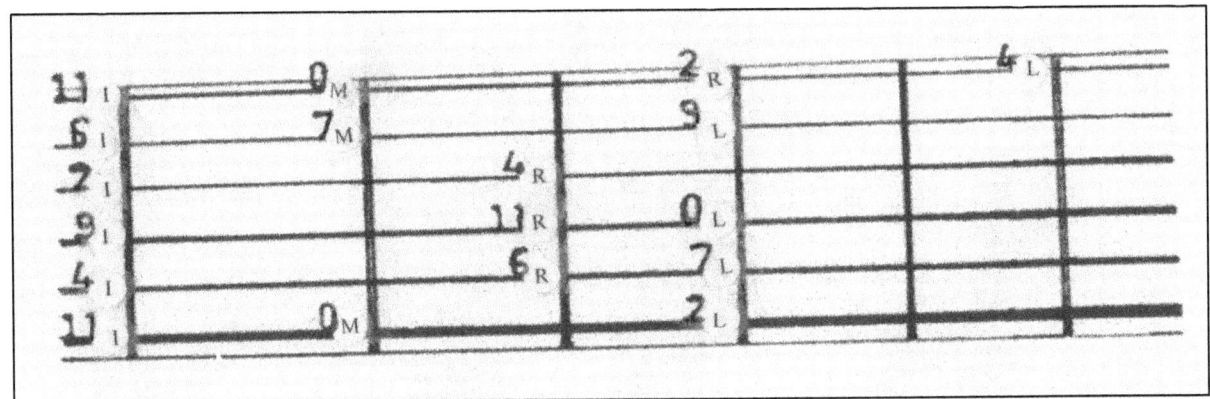

Mode Four

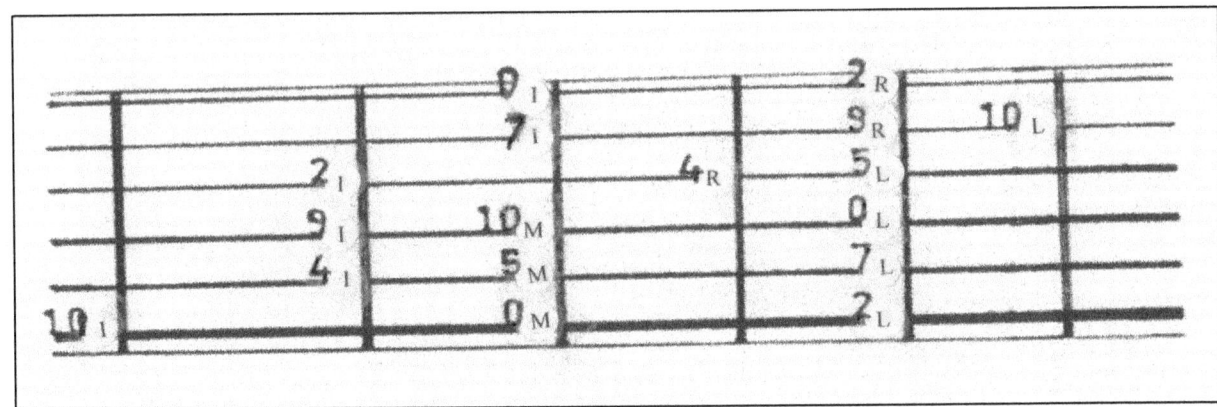

Mode Five

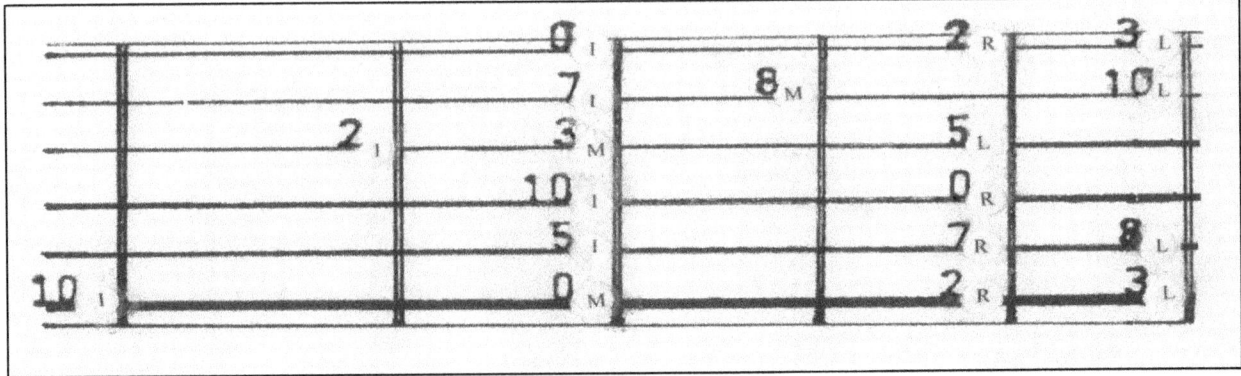

Mode Six

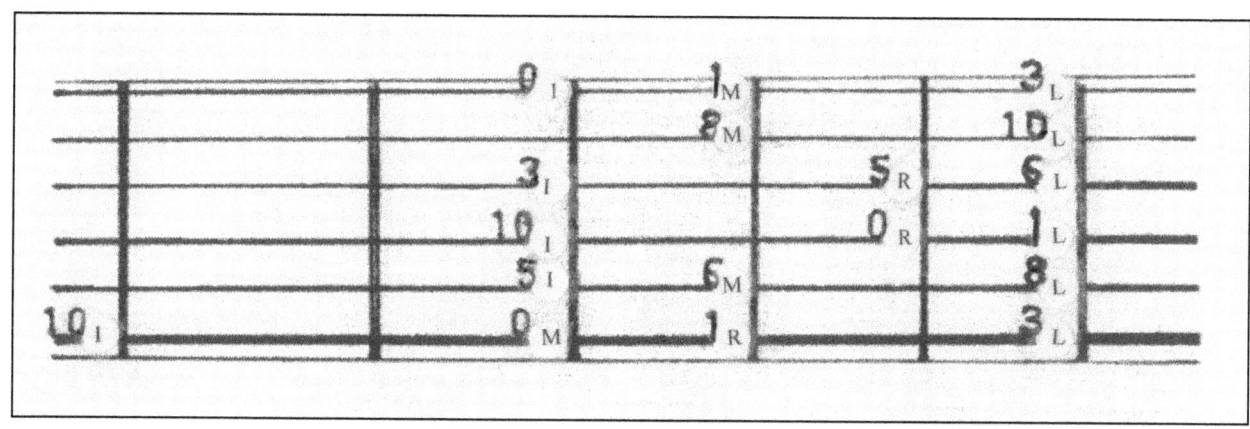

Mode Seven

In the next diagram we arrive back at Mode One.

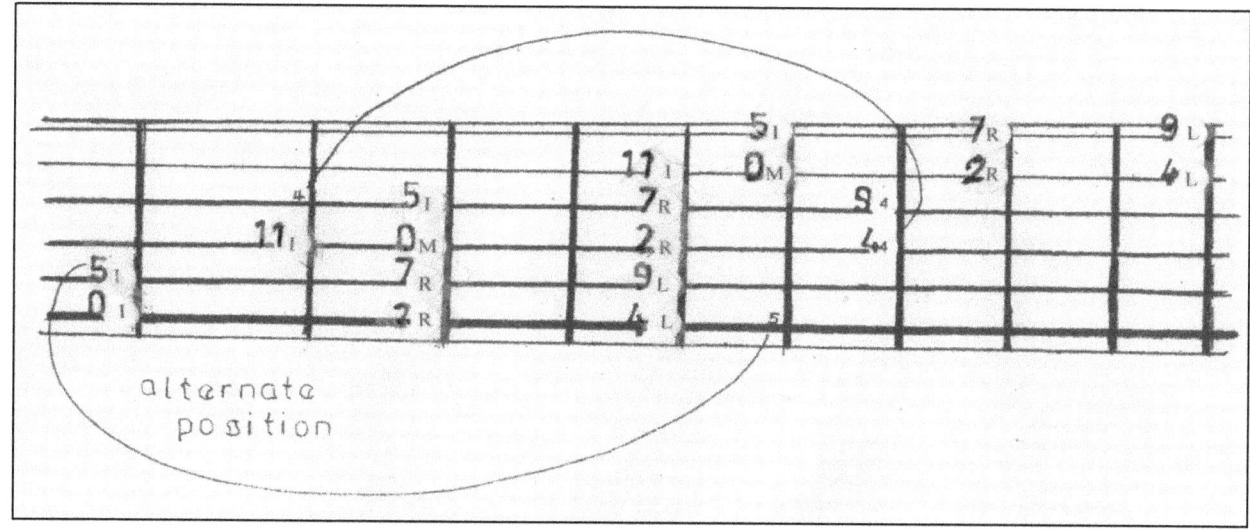

Mode One

From the preceding diagrams we can imagine what would happen if we were to go outside of the box and make changes to the original modes. There is quite a gamut. Some are modified with only a changed single note. Still others are hybrids of hybrids. It will be fun to learn the Pentatonic Scale, fundamental to rock and roll and the blues. There is a chart at the end of this section listing the covered scales with their Music Numbers. Modes and their variations are all open to creativeness within.

<< BOOGIE WOOGIE >>

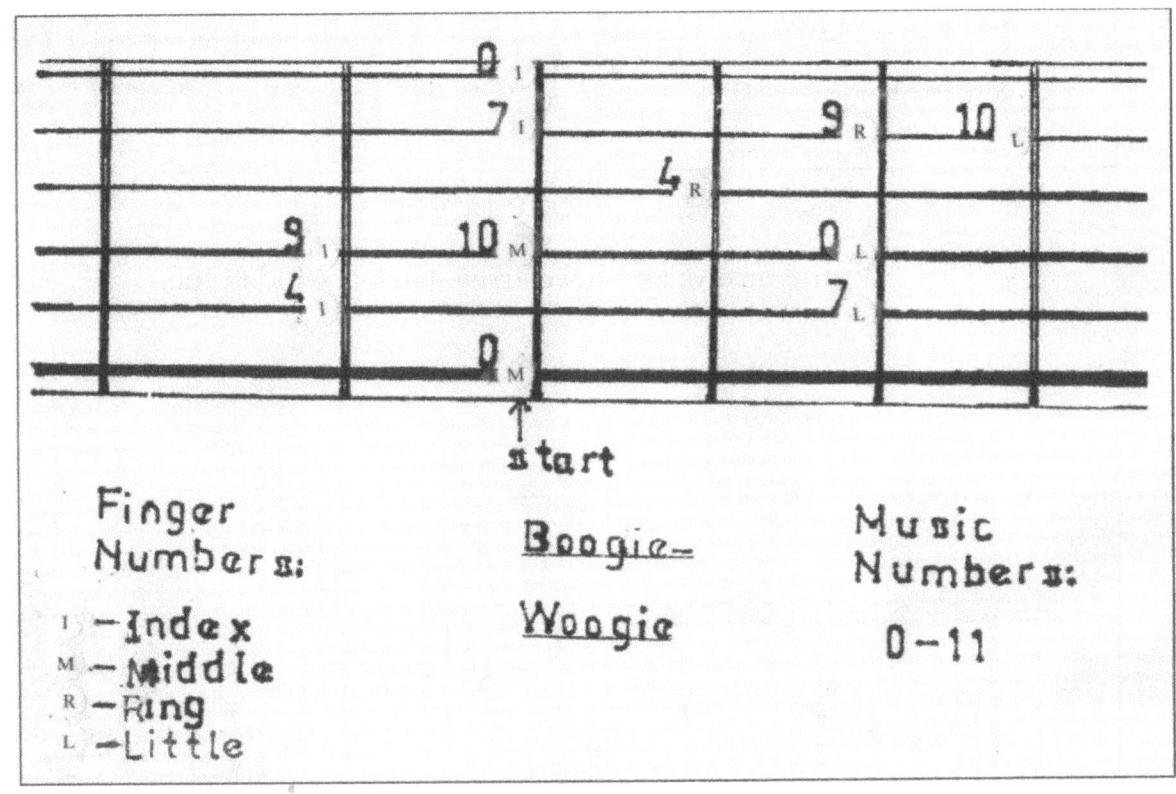

Boogie Woogie Scale: 0-4-7-9-10

<< PENTATONIC SCALE >>
(basic to rock and roll and the Blues)

Basic Pentatonic MNs are: 0-3-5-7-10. We'll transform the Pentatonic (five note) scale into the major Blues pattern by adding the MN note 6.

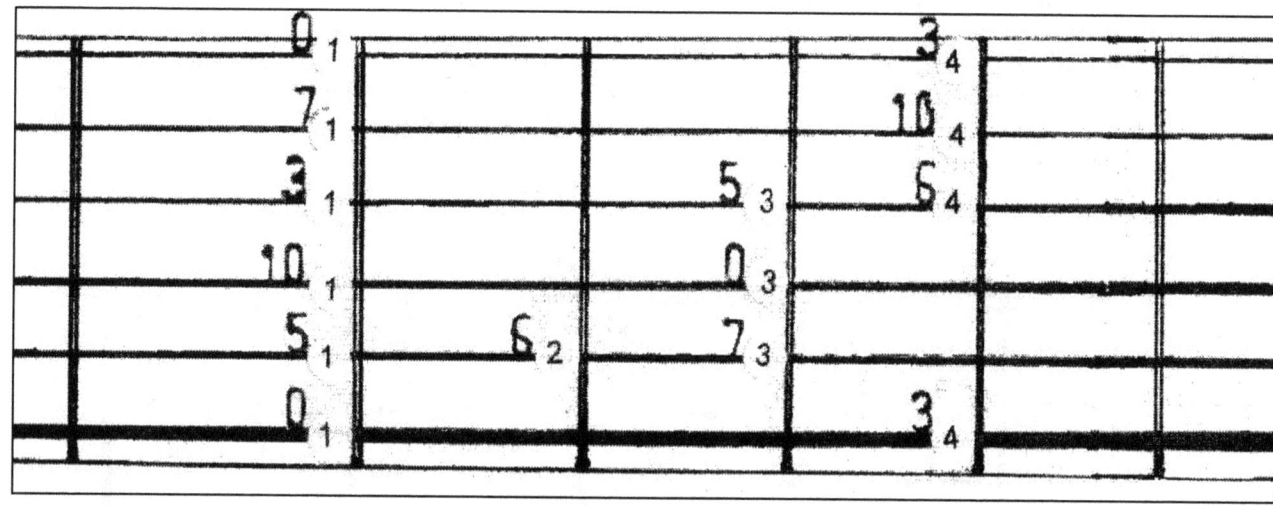

THE BLUES
Pentatonic Position One (+ Blues Note no. 6)

As we derived other modes from Mode One, we can also derive positions for the Pentatonic Scale.

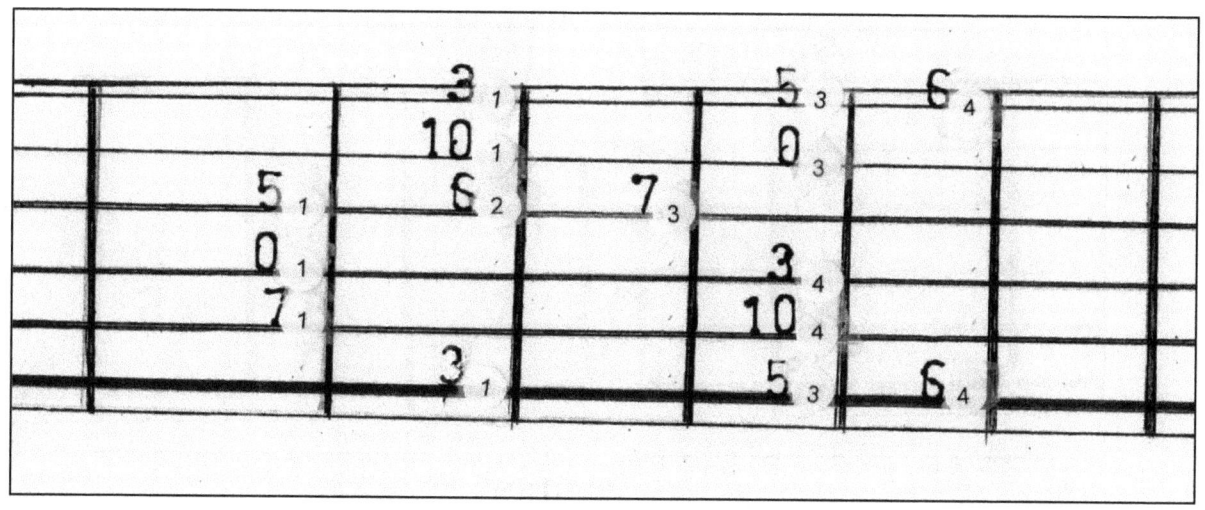

Position Two

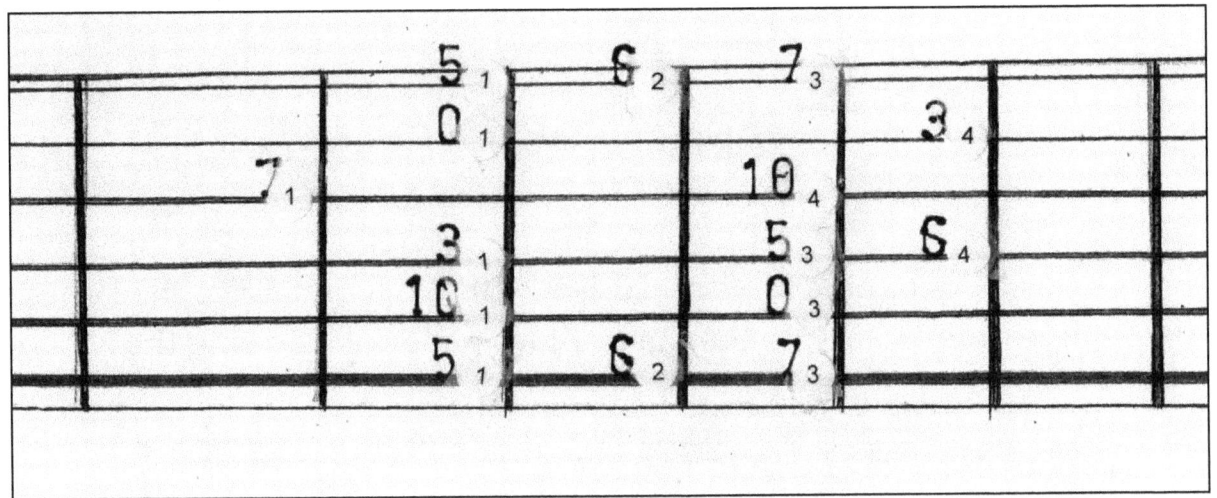

Position Three

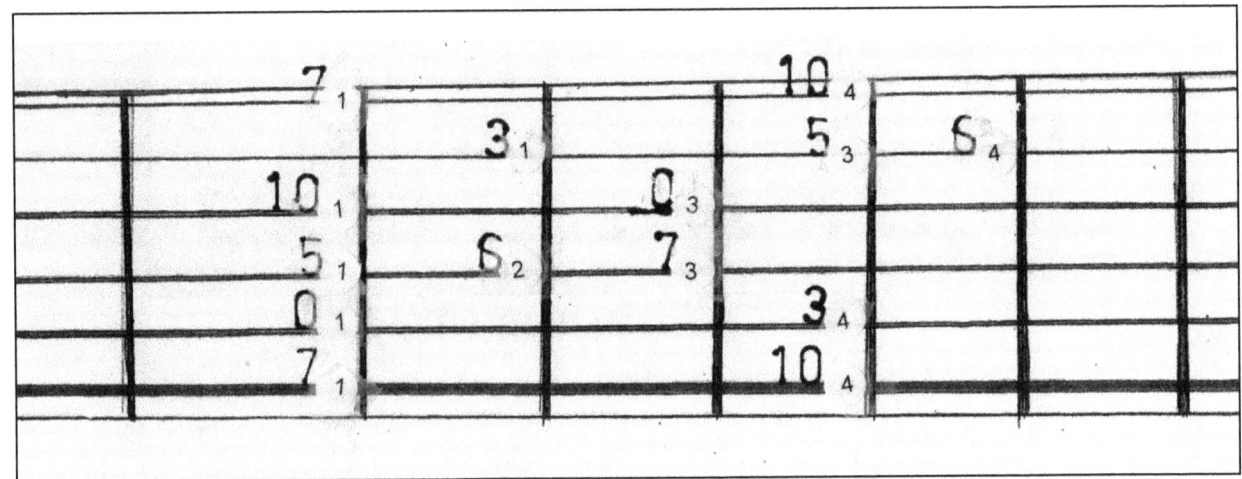

Position Four

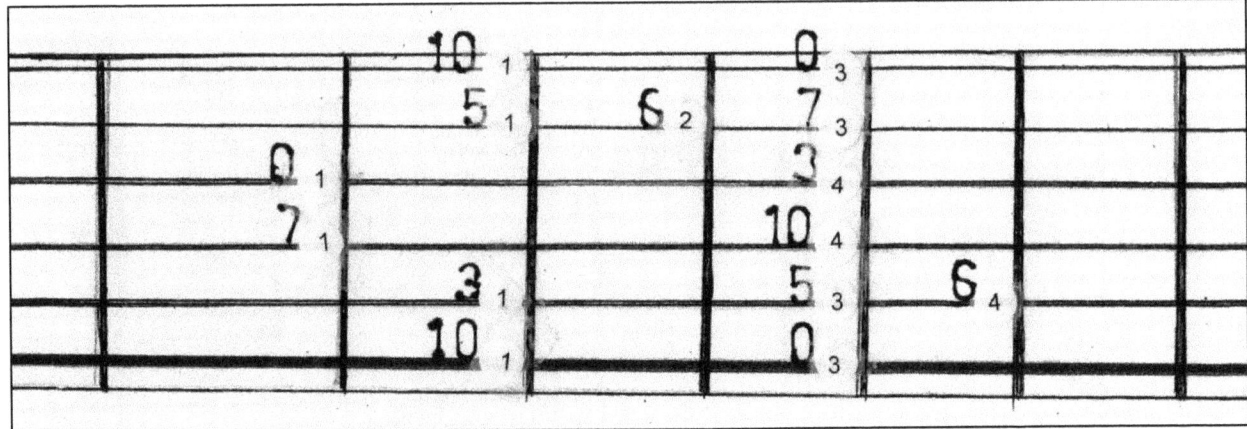

Position Five

<< GUITAR/KEYBOARD CORRELATION >>

The following diagram correlates the open strings of the guitar with the keys on a keyboard. Notice how the keyboard keys match the guitar frets note for note. Good Luck on your continuing studies empowered with Music Numbers.

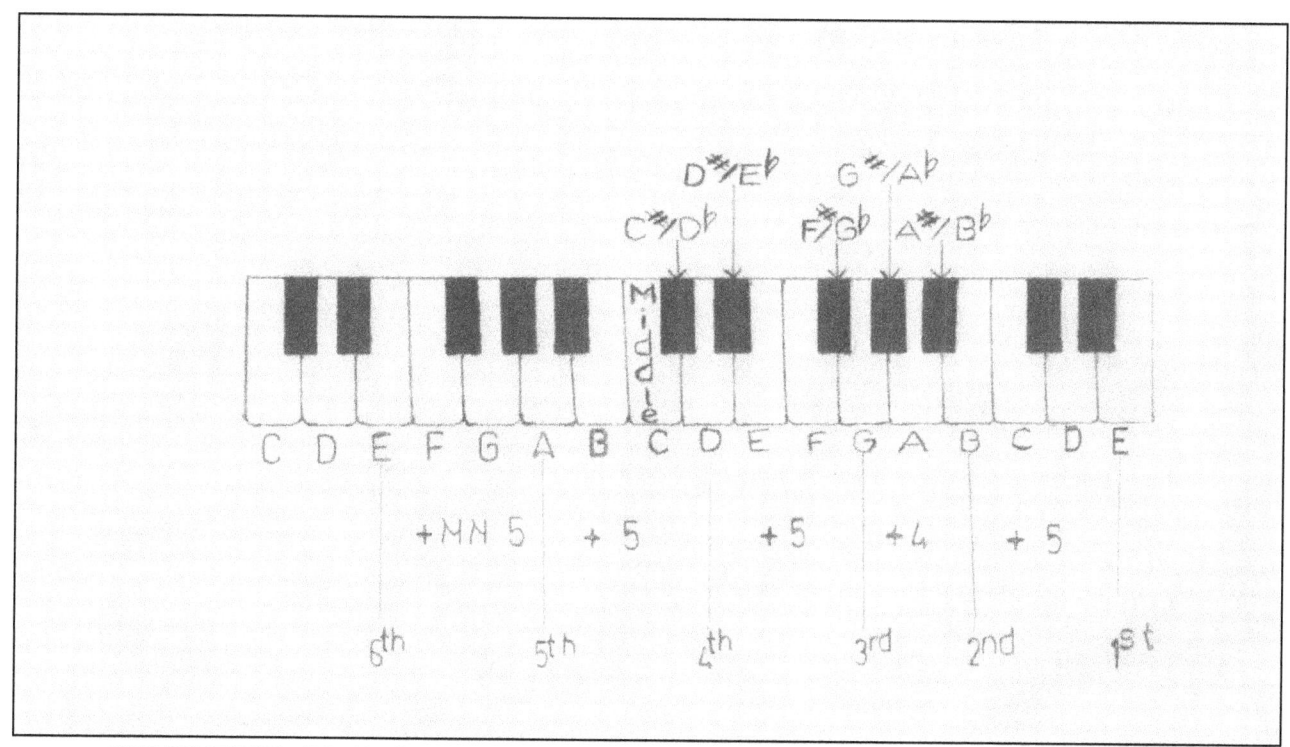

HOW THE GUITAR STRINGS CORRELATE TO THE KEYBOARD

« LIST of SCALE CODES »

Mode One..........................0-2-4-5-7-9-11
Mode Two.........................0-2-3-5-7-9-10
Mode Three......................0-1-3-5-7-8-10
Mode Four........................0-2-4-6-7-9-11
Mode Five.........................0-2-4-5-7-9-10
Mode Six...........................0-2-3-5-7-8-10
Mode Seven.....................0-1-3-5-6-8-10
Boogie-Woogie.................0-4-7-9-10
Pentatonic........................0-3-5-7-10
Blues.................................0-3-5-6-7-10

My name is Shanny; thank you for reading my book.

Shannyelk005@shaw.ca
Or
www.shannysplace.com